The Now What Guide:
Planning Your Education (and Life) After High School

Juliana Christine Griffo

THE NOW WHAT GUIDE

Planning Your Education (and Life) After High School

Juliana Christine Griffo

Last Plutonian, L.L.C.

Copyright © 2022 Juliana Christine Griffo

Published via Amazon by Last Plutonian, L.L.C.

All rights reserved.

No part of this book may be reproduced, or stored in a retrieval system, or transmitted in any form or by any means, electronic, mechanical, photocopying, recording, or otherwise, without express written permission of the publisher.

ISBN: 978-1-7355237-4-3

Cover design by: Caitlyn Ryan
Manuscript edit by: Tyran Grillo
Audiobook edit by: Leif Grant

Printed in the United States of America

I wrote this book for YOU!

*In Loving Memory of My Mother
Joanne Griffo
Media Specialist and Retired High School Librarian*

Mom, I'm still sorry for "works in a library" getting into that article all these years later. I have always known it was an important job and I can include it in these books now, but only because I saw you demonstrating the value of it all for 38 years.

"NOW WHAT?"

The Clueless Student's Guide to College Applications, Choosing Where to Go, and What to Study

By Juliana Griffo

Published by Last Plutonian, L.L.C.

Introduction: How to use this guide effectively

Chapter 1: Academia: Is it for you?

Chapter 2: Home Life: Controlling, abusive, and/or helicopter parents and other environmental pressures

Chapter 3: Finances: What can you afford?

Chapter 4: Asking for a Friend: How to find out what the school you're considering is REALLY like

Chapter 5: Areas of Study: Interests for majors, minors, and graduate tracks

Chapter 6: Public or Private College or University: What matters for what you're interested in doing?

Chapter 7: Applications: How to decide which schools to apply for

Chapter 8: Personal Essays: How to write the best personal statements and application material possible

Chapter 9: Managing Expectations: What to do while waiting for answers

Chapter 10: Scholarships/Grants/Financial Aid: How to find and apply to the most helpful sources of money for you

Chapter 11: What's Next: Preparing for college (Bonus Chapter)

Introduction: How to use this guide effectively

I wrote this book for many situations. It leans heavily toward going on to higher education after high school, but I don't want anybody who picks this book up to think that only those bound for college will benefit from it. Neither would I want my readers to think of college as the be-all and end-all of their existence. College is a huge investment, and I'm not just talking financially. College will regularly siphon your energy and turn your brain into mush, and if you aren't fully interested and committed to what you're there to do, it's a horrible form of self-harm that nobody should have to endure. That might not sound like what you'd expect in a book about what to do after high school and how to get into higher education, but if I told you that you *needed* college to have a good life, I'd be a liar. And I'm not a liar.

I want you to use this book to self-assess. What is it that *you* want out of life? How can you get there? The answers are not in this book. What you will find here is how to *get to* the answers. The answers are your own. I want you to feel as in control as possible of your life, even when plenty of factors are out of your control, as they are for everyone (this is the nature of human existence). If you want to go live on a self-sustaining, fully green farm for the rest of your days, there's likely government assistance, grants, training, and cheap land you can save up for and get started on right out of high school—but if you need to apply for assistance or training, this book will help. If at any point you need to self-assess and construct a plan for yourself, search for resources, or ask for help, let the following pages be your compass. If you have an extremely specific and "nontraditional" dream, I hope you borrow this book from the library or a friend because I did write it with a broad audience in mind.

You don't need to read this book precisely in chapter order to get value from it. If you've already worked out that you want to go to college, the necessary budgeting and finances, and which colleges you want to apply for, you will still find chapters 8 through 11 helpful, and it is probably worthwhile spending some time reading other chapters related to finances and budgeting.

I'm writing *for you*. Yes, you, the unknown person in possession of some form of this book, be it digital, physical, or audio. I want you to be able to take this huge question of "What do I do with my life?" and feel like you have a traversable path forward in figuring that out. I don't think this book will solve all your problems or bring about world peace, but I hope it can ease the planning process regarding training or education and bring about some peace for *you*. A calm, logical approach to creating a plan and deciding what you want to do will help you through any life event at any point, so learning to apply this skill to training should inform any "What do I do now?" questions you have in the future.

CHAPTER 1: ACADEMIA: IS IT FOR YOU?

What is academia? Try this little exercise.

What do you think of when you hear the word "academia"? I'll wait. Seriously. Take a few minutes and think about it. Write it down if you feel motivated.

Finished? Great!

Unfortunately, there's no way you can think of everything that fits inside the vast sinkhole of the term "academia." Just mentioning "academia" this many times in the same few sentences is obnoxious and makes me hate myself.

You'll never really know what "academia" is *really* like until you're out of high school and firmly entrenched in the muddy goop that is higher education. It's also hugely different from school to school, program to program, so it's downright impossible to describe.

I'm going to break down some basic aspects of it for you as best I can anyway.

College or University: What's the difference?

Simplest answer: Whereas "college" generally refers to smaller campuses geared toward undergraduate programs, "university" refers to larger campuses supporting both undergraduate and graduate programs. They are all similarly accredited.

Any decisions you make about attending a college or university should be based on the individual school, not these words, but I'll try to list some quick pros and cons.

If you're at a university, you'll have more access to advanced courses, have a somewhat better chance of getting into a graduate program (because you'll already be on track course-wise) and a chance at a bigger network of peers, which is especially worthwhile if you are choosing a creative or technical track where knowing people to team up with is crucial. A university will also offer a bigger sea of students to compete with, the potential of a larger student-to-professor ratio, and enough space to make it difficult (if not impossible) to get from one side of campus to the other in time for classes.

Being at a college has the opposite pros and cons. You'll have far less competition, better access to less-stretched professors, and plenty of time to get from one class to another. If you're doing undergraduate work to get into a special graduate program, you likely won't have the advantage of simply moving up within your school system. You'll have fewer classmates, so you'll be able to get to know them better, though your reputation, whether good or bad, will follow you around more closely. You'll have fewer advanced courses to choose from because there won't be a graduate-level program supporting allowing advanced undergraduates to attend.

At the end of the day, these are generalizations and barely touch on what's important to consider about academia and whether it's right for you.

Campus Life: On or off campus?

The *culture* of a school will vary based on whether you're living on campus or off and whether you attend virtually or are local. When attending school virtually, you miss out on some of the perks of being there in person. This isn't a big issue, however, if you're busy juggling numerous other things in life, such as raising children or a full-time job, and you need this degree for something you've already got lined up. You may be looking to pursue a specific degree because your job requires you to have one in hand to promote you, as sometimes happens. Because virtual programs tend to be *just about getting the requirements done*, this path is not for everyone and is only a small part of what academia is. The bright side of attending an online-only school is that the school may prioritize providing online extracurriculars or opportunities to students, though some opportunities will be impossible to engage in virtually.

Living on campus has plenty of pros and cons, depending on your personality. Living on campus will change your experience of "academia." Living on campus subjects you to the general culture of the student body. If the school is a "party school," meaning there are frequent parties or Greek life is a huge part of many students' lives, it'll be very different from a campus where the tone is much more serious. Living on campus means eating in the dining hall, sharing bathrooms and dorm rooms, trying not to be the annoying person in the building making noise at 3 a.m. (or trying to find and silence the person in the building making noise at 3 a.m.), and choosing from among the many distractions, temptations, and fun things to do.

Living off campus is partly like living on campus but offers benefits like privacy and independence from strict dorm rules. There are downsides to being off campus, like commuting to campus for classes and being much farther away from class if you're running late. It's also harder to make and maintain friendships and connections because you might not be as easily able to bond or get together for a project. You'll have less time in the day to be productive if you're commuting, too, especially if you have to park a car in a packed campus parking lot.

Theory vs. Practice

Different schools will have a "culture" that focuses efforts differently. The school's focus might be on theory or it might emphasize hands-on experience. A research lab, for example, will have a different focus than a lab that aims to produce something. Campuses will likely be a blend both of these things, so that the philosophy department will have different goals than a medical research lab.

The "culture" of academia that you experience in school will depend on your goals. One of my friends from college did a lot of research in the science lab to pursue his Ph.D. The atmosphere was very different for him than for me in graduate school—my MFA was in Interactive Media, and I spent my three years in that program producing content. He spent his years (longer than me!) doing something with viruses and assays that, to this day, I still don't fully understand. His professors treated students and their work differently from mine. My professors needed to provide feedback on the games and experiences that I produced, while his professors were mentoring him in research methods.

Academia is generally the world of studying rather than the "real world," per se. The "real world" is a phrase I'm sure you've heard more times than you can count, but I'm not sure it should be weaponized as much as it seems to be. The "real world" is, in many ways, simpler than the academic world, though we often hear as students that it's the other way around. I wish we just said that experiences outside of school are different and stopped making it such a huge source of anxiety.

That said, academia is not for the faint-hearted or anyone who doesn't like to study, research, and put in a lot of effort. Whether you dedicate your life to academia and "studying" or you study what you need and launch into your life and career depends on what you intend to do in school. No matter what path you take in higher education, whether it's more research-oriented or production-oriented, you *will* need to "study."

Culture

We use "culture" to apply to everything nowadays, but the word still applies here. Different cultures abound on every campus, in each program, and in each school within a college or university. Despite sounding more like a keyword than a real thing you should care about, it's going to be important to find a place that you feel comfortable being in. No amount of ambition to learn can overcome the total misery of being in a place you don't like.

I'll tell you now about my experience in undergraduate and graduate school in relation to "culture." I wasn't very happy as an undergrad. For one thing, it snowed most of the damn year, and slogging through the snow or rain or mix of garbage got old fast. Moreover, my high school was a diverse regional school. My bloodline is 100% Sicilian—my whole family comes from that little island that Italy's boot is shaking off. Being Italian American in the town I grew up in wasn't super, but it was fine when I went to the high school where (of the three) most of my town wouldn't send their kids. In my high school, you didn't hear only English in the halls; you heard a lot of languages. I was a minority. I loved it.

In undergrad, the campus was almost all white—not my Italian "white" but *white* white. Everyone looked the same to me, and it seemed that most everyone was from a rich family. My beloved Toyota Celica, which was almost my age, was a popular target for vandals. I once found footprints in the snow *over* my car—marks and scratches that remained until the last day I drove it. They *walked over my car.* They destroyed my radio antenna several times. In my classes, particularly sociology (which I particularly enjoyed) and one juvenile delinquency class, my fellow students discussed the terrible things they had gotten away with in high school, including drinking and driving, vandalism, theft, drugs—all things that we in my high school would never even have considered doing since we were often the ones getting in trouble for things that paled in comparison. (For example, the police wanted to arrest seniors for a prank that involved stealing all the pumpkins in the area the day after Halloween and arranging them around the flagpole outside the school.) My sociology classmates discussed smashing mailboxes from car windows with a baseball bat and getting away with it, even talking to police and being let off simply because they were "just being teenagers."

I was able to finish in three and a half years, even with a leave of absence, and I had no regrets about finishing sooner rather than later. I wasn't happy with the school's culture, and the only saving grace was that I was very fond of one of my professors, who I had for most of my core classes. She was the only reason

I returned to that school. I did meet other professors I appreciated, but you can understand my point: It matters where you go, but it also matters who will be around you.

Hard Work

If you weren't aware, I've already published a book called *The Lazy Student's Guide to Writing Papers and Getting College Done Right: Work Smarter, Not Harder*. While there's plenty of important stuff in there that won't appear in this book, one sentiment I can't help but repeat here is that you *will* have to work in school. The trick is to work the right amount of "hard." The new subject matter won't be easy, the hands-on experience won't be easy, balancing work/school and life won't be easy…but if you're willing to put in the effort, you won't have to sell your soul in the process. The hard work will come in when you're trying to establish and maintain self-care, time management, and a good work ethic. Academic life requires you to learn how to prioritize and be efficient. If you aren't interested in being efficient and performing the mental labor of deciding what you will and won't do and when, academic life might not be for you. You'll need to have a strong sense of independence and self-reliance.

CHAPTER 2: HOME LIFE: CONTROLLING, ABUSIVE, AND/ OR HELICOPTER PARENTS AND OTHER ENVIRONMENTAL PRESSURES

An important thing you'll need to self-assess is how to deal with pressures you have little to no control over and how they might affect your choices relating to higher education. I'm not a therapist, doctor, or professional qualified to give legal advice. I'm simply someone with experience. It's up to you whether the following advice applies to you and whether you want to take it to heart.

With my disclaimer out of the way, let me start by describing some of the pressures and issues that can affect your decisions surrounding colleges and life paths.

Financial Aid

If you don't have a college fund or trust fund ready to pay for anything you want to do, then financial aid will affect you for any amount of schooling. Financial aid is a lot of hoops to jump through, carries tons of risk, and will likely never stop being a headache until college is free for everyone. There are scholarships and grants, but those are not easy to win when so many compete for them, and even if you do get them, they generally tack on pressure from requirements to keep them. Accept that you will need to figure out a good fit for you based on money, but also accept that it's okay to find this frustrating in light of your biggest goals. You just need to cast a wider search net to find what's right for you.

If you have controlling parents who are holding your financial aid hostage because of your age (financial aid needs you to be older to be considered independent in general in the United States) or otherwise dangling money over your head to force you into decisions, financial aid can seem like a dirty word. Before I help you with that problem, there's something we need to talk about. The following section may be difficult going, but bear with me.

Controlling Parents/Guardians or "Helicopter" Parents/Guardians

Even the healthiest of families will probably produce a teenager who looks at the decisions ahead of them after graduating high school with a bit of anxiety about what their parents might think. I'm talking, however, about the budding students who look at college and think they might like a specific path, but their parents have other plans for them, and the backlash of even remotely hinting at what the teenager wants is huge. Controlling parents who insist you join a specific sport or club you have no interest in do not, in fact, have your best interests in mind. What you have to understand is that they most likely *believe* they do.

Helicopter parents have probably spent your entire life "hovering" over everything you do, either micromanaging or removing any sense of privacy or individuality you have so that they can continue to have control over you as you grow. This is often disguised as wanting the best for their child, but they really just end up smothering and pushing their children away when they become adults.

Abusive/Neglectful Parents/Guardians

There are several types of child abuse, and only a few of them are ever spoken about with a sense of certainty.

Physical abuse: A parent or guardian physically harms/attacks you with or without any discernable reason (and, as the minor in the situation, it is *never* your fault). While this type of abuse tends to reduce in frequency as a child ages and becomes more physically capable of self-defense, this can go on well into adulthood and is incredibly damaging emotionally. However, physical abuse typically leaves marks. Often, by the time a child is a teenager, they've been able to show proof to someone that they are being abused because there are witnessable signs of this abuse.

Sexual abuse: A parent or guardian sexually assaults, grooms, allows a child to be sexually assaulted or groomed, pimps, or otherwise makes a child uncomfortable with their body. This can leave some marks or signs that serve as "proof" of a child's story. All too often, children and teenagers, especially boys and young men, are unable to bring themselves to seek help, and so, the abuse continues silently. Sexual abuse can be difficult to recognize since it takes many forms, some of which might seem normal without all the details. A quintessential example goes something like this: A stepfather joins the family when the stepdaughter is 13 years old. At first, nothing happens, but by the time the stepdaughter is 16, the stepfather is regularly making comments about what she's wearing and pointing out her breasts frequently. Instead of saying, "Hey, don't wear that tank top to the mall; it's very revealing," as any concerned parent might, he says, "You need to change that tank top because I don't want anyone else looking at your breasts. I think they've gotten bigger this week. Is it that point in your cycle?" Such sexual abuse can be difficult to recognize and explain to others. Obviously, if the stepfather gets into the stepdaughter's bed at night and holds her down and forces her, it's rape. This type of abuse can be so confusing, though, that victims aren't even sure who to tell and might even be blamed for the abuse—maybe the mom in this situation doesn't believe her daughter and sides with the stepfather. Now, what happens to this 16-year-old?

Neglect: A parent or guardian fails, for a wide variety of reasons, to provide even basic needs to a child. Children who lack three square meals, appropriate apparel for the season, shoes, shelter, clean water, medical care, or furniture are being neglected. Neglect that is intentional is included in other types of abuse, too. All sorts of toxic parents are capable of neglect. Even good-intentioned, loving parents can walk the line of neglect, perhaps if they are very poor or have a lot of children within the same narrow age group.

Emotional/Mental abuse: A parent or guardian engages in any variety of behavior that leaves a child emotionally hurting. This has so many facets that it's almost too difficult to define in one paragraph. It could be bullying, favoritism among siblings, scapegoating, controlling, criticizing, not teaching basic skills appropriate to a child's age, forcing a child to walk on eggshells for fear of anger or guilt, burdening a child with adult issues (one parent discussing intimate relationship issues with the child as a support, for example), or silent treatment. There are many more examples of emotional abuse. Too few rules or too many rules can create anxiety, stress, and depression in a child. Treating a child as an extension of oneself or property also falls into this category. Telling a child there are children in the world who have it worse and insisting the child be thankful that things aren't worse instead of addressing a child's trauma and validating a child's emotions is also hurtful. Parents or guardians guilty of this type of abuse (not a parent who might accidentally miss a child's emotional signals or who can be a little strict about age-appropriate chores or consequences for legitimately bad behavior) often have personality disorders like narcissism or are addicts. While an addict can seek rehabilitation and healing for the sake of their child or children, a true narcissist is unable to change and often fools the world around them, leaving the child firmly alone in this abuse. It is much less difficult for a teacher to notice that a child isn't wearing a winter coat when it's freezing and snowing out than it is to notice that a child feels unsafe at home and mentally tormented. Resilient kids learn that they should never allow anyone else to see the abusive behavior long before they actually understand that what is happening to them is abusive behavior. This makes it extremely difficult to report and for Child Protective Services to do anything about it.

Medical abuse: This is usually very difficult to spot as an outsider. Medical abuse involves a parent or guardian refusing to seek appropriate medical care for a child. This also includes making a child sick, as in factitious disorder imposed on another, or FDIA— formerly known as Munchausen syndrome by proxy. This includes guardians who don't believe in allergies refusing to treat a child with severe reactions to nature and refusing gynecological care to a child with painful or irregular periods. If your guardian once took an hour to figure out what to do about your broken arm in the middle of the woods, this would not fall into this category. Neither is it necessarily inappropriate that a guardian seeks out alternative care for a child, so long as there is an effective treatment that is not harming or depriving a child. This means that administering some helpful herb for a viral cold that a regular doctor wouldn't prescribe any medication for wouldn't count as medical abuse. However, using the same herbal remedy to treat a large cancerous tumor in lieu of surgically removing the tumor would be medical abuse. This category can also include preventing/denying access to mental health services and/or denying that mental health issues exist.

Financial abuse: This can get super complicated as well and includes, but is in no way limited to, holding the promise of funds over someone's head. For abused children, this will often look like turning 18 and being kicked out, asked for rent, handed a bill for all the costs the child has incurred since being born (including the hospital bills for pregnancy and being born), and, when it comes to college, "If you go to [parent's preferred school] and study [parent's desired field], I will pay for it. Otherwise, you'll need to take huge loans and live on your own, and I won't support you." If any of this sounds unfamiliar, you probably haven't been financially abused, but if it does, I feel for you.

The abuse you probably know about and can most easily detect? Well, spotting bruises is usually how physical abuse comes to light and children are believed. A child freezing without a coat or being severely malnourished is moderately likely to be noticed and believed (depending on the signs of the neglect, of course). Sexual abuse is probably equally as believed as neglect depending on the actual signs—a pregnant 12-year-old girl is clearly the victim of sexual abuse, though plenty of situations are muddied, secret, and difficult to detect. And while the forms of abuse I've outlined above are those that society generally can handle recognizing, all types of child abuse can slip through the cracks, be difficult to detect, and usually involve the victim feeling afraid of and guilty about this secret.

How to Recognize What You're Fighting

So, you're probably wondering why I listed types of child abuse in a book about getting into college. The thing is, no matter how well adjusted you might be and how functional and loving your family is, at least some of this stuff is likely to resonate with you. A family with good intentions can still put a lot of pressure and stress on you and resort to unhealthy behaviors related to your life choices. If your family *is* toxic, then you'll need some extra strategies for figuring out what it is they're doing and how to deal with it.

Questions to ask yourself:

1. Have I ever been physically abused?

2. Have I ever been sexually abused?

3. Did I always have adequate clothing, shelter, food and water, access to healthcare, and school supplies while growing up?

4. Have I ever had guilt or pressure relating to paying to live before turning 18?

5. Were hugs and emotional validation freely given in my household?

If you can answer "No, no, yes, no, and yes" to these five questions, then the chances are that any negative incidents in your childhood were isolated, meaning that your risk of being a child abuse victim is low. If a few of them are the "wrong" answer, you've probably got some childhood trauma to deal with as you move into becoming an adult. I'm not a psychologist, and you certainly could still have been abused and still answered these five questions "right." If so, your experiences are valid. Even if you weren't abused growing up, there could be plenty of stress and guilt surrounding your next steps in life that feel dangerously close to abuse.

Let's figure out some coping mechanisms together.

If You Are in an Abusive Environment

I hate to be the bearer of bad news, but you have some tough stuff to get through ahead of you if you fall into this category. Almost no one has grown up in a perfectly healthy environment for the entirety of their childhood. While it might feel defeating to be in a toxic or abusive environment, there's also good news.

Now you can recognize it and work to deal with it. I'm not a religious person and wouldn't push religion on you even if I was, but there's a chapter (number 71, to be precise) in the *Tao Te Ching* (which is philosophy to me but can also be religious and spiritual) that says:

> Knowing you don't know is wholeness.
>
> Thinking you know is a disease.
>
> Only by recognizing that you have an illness can you move to seek a cure.
>
> The Master is whole because
> she sees her illnesses and treats them,
> and thus is able to remain whole.

This chapter has been translated many times over thousands of years from classical Chinese, so there are plenty of variations out there, but I like this one the most because the message comes out clearest to me.

The first and most overarching coping

mechanism for toxic environments is to recognize what's happening. If you recognize what's going on, that you're being pressured or manipulated, it's a lot easier to prevent that manipulation from messing with your life plans. The more you recognize toxic external factors, the more easily you can remind yourself of being able to only control *your* actions, which is another vital coping mechanism.

You can't change other people, and you can't control other people, but you can choose to remove yourself from a toxic situation or ignore others' hurtful behavior. Does this always work perfectly to the point where you no longer ever feel bad? Of course not, but it's definitely better than wrestling with even naming the negative feelings and stressors that are affecting you, adding confusion to your life.

You *can* control making a plan for your life, which is what this guide is for, so you're already taking a step in that direction. Coping mechanisms also include therapy, speaking to a guidance counselor, self-care, and socializing with good friends. If you know you are a victim of child abuse and need an escape plan to find safety and relief, you might even consider finding ways to leave and be safe *right now*, even if you're not quite ready for college or legally old enough to be an adult. You can ask for help at school or from a guidance counselor, a trusted adult, or a doctor. You can even call hotlines for child abuse or call Child Protective Services for yourself.

For the rest of this book, I'm not going to harp on

abuse, but if you're currently being abused, don't act on the advice of this guide until you have a safe, solid plan in place. If you feel you are unsafe to remain in your living situation, see assistance immediately in crafting a safe escape plan: it may not be safe to just walk out the door while an abuser is home or it may be the best time to walk out and you'll need help to navigate that.

Before I end this chapter and move on to the next about finances, I want to mention that it *is* possible to get financial aid without your parents or guardians under some extreme circumstances. If you have proof of physical or sexual abuse, you can usually provide this and obtain financial aid without their finances. If you have already become emancipated, the same rule applies. If you have a parent or guardian who is refusing to respond or you have no way to contact, this *may* be an excuse to be assessed without their finances. Contact your target school or schools and ask the financial aid office directly about these scenarios. Obviously, if one or both parents or any of your guardians pass away, you need to show that they are deceased.

The takeaway from this chapter, whether you're in a toxic environment or a functional one, is that as you move into adulthood, your decisions must be your own. Any pressure from others is something you should never allow to sway the plans you are forming in any direction that you aren't 100% passionate about.

CHAPTER 3: FINANCES: WHAT CAN YOU AFFORD?

It's time for some math. In an ideal world, there'd be no money and the economy would be based entirely on resources. Completely equal and essentially a paradise. Sadly, people with power like to keep it, so don't count on that paradise happening anytime soon before you make your first adult plans.

First, I want to talk about how crucial it is to be as creative and resourceful as you can be *right now*. You're thinking of things you'd like to do with your life and analyzing them in a very critical manner. What do you want to do as an adult? What are your long-term goals? No matter what they are right now, even if they're fuzzy and essentially non-existent, you will need to find ways to financially support yourself.

Ideally, you'd have already been working, saving, and investing. If you haven't, don't stress about it; just add it to your plans now. Remember to take into account any resources that you might have access to upon graduating that you didn't have access to before finishing high school, such as a college fund, trust fund, or some inheritance. It's also possible that you might have some savings bonds from when you were born. Now's the time to ask your parents or guardians about such sources of funding and any stipulations that may come with them. A savings bond might be a 30-year bond, meaning it won't fully mature for thirty years from the date it was purchased. For example, my grandmother purchased savings bonds for me starting from the day I was born and continuing on through graduating high school. She was shy of 74 years old when I was born and a practical woman, so she even set aside bonds for other occasions, figuring that she might be gone before then but that these bonds would be there anyway. She passed at just shy of 106 years old, and the 30-year bond she purchased for me still has a few more years to full maturity. I am in my thirties and only now able to cash fully matured bonds. Not all bonds are 30-year bonds, of course, so that just means it is possible that other types of bonds might have been purchased for you and are matured now or will be in the near future.

If you are fortunate enough to have a college fund, trust fund, inheritance, or some other specialized source of funding, check into the details of this money to see whether it stipulates that the money be used for school or has any other stipulations about receiving the money related to your age or use of the money.

When I went about writing my will, then updating it after moving to a different state, I stipulated that some money would go to the special children in my life—I am not a parent and have no siblings, but I grew up with two of my first cousins, who have children. Some of my closest friends also have children I am close with. The will-making software I used forced me into stipulating that there be a trust for any minors and that those minors would not be able to get access to this money until they reached a certain age. Hopefully, I won't die anytime soon and can be around to give them that money, but just setting up any gift required me to provide some stipulations. All sources of potential funding must be well researched so that you can be sure of obtaining and using the money you are counting on.

Next, where are you living, and where do you want to live? If you are fortunate enough to have parents who will financially support you while you go to school, then you still need to make a plan right now that starts to capitalize on that advantage. At some point, you want to be ready to live independently, so no matter what advantages you have, use them wisely.

If you don't have any financial assistance or support from your family but want to go to school for something (more on what this could be later), you'll need to call the financial aid office at any institution you're interested in applying to and attending. You might be able to get some scholarships or grants, and you obviously should look for those, too, but when getting the numbers from financial aid offices, assume you have zero dollars coming to you. This will help you make decisions that don't leave you in stressful limbo because that limbo will easily hinder you from keeping all the balls you're juggling in the air at once.

How much is a degree going to cost? Make sure that number covers rent/food/life for the entire time it will take you to get the degree. Also, be sure to recognize that you might take more or less time to complete the degree than the average. I took a semester off from undergraduate school and completed my degree in three and a half years. I had a bit of summer credit to speed things up, but mostly I had credit rollover from AP classes and the six credits (two classes) I took during my senior year of high school at the local university as part of a special program. In hindsight, this saved me some money, even if that wasn't my intention at the time. My graduate degree was a special program that could only be completed in order across three years (no more, no less). That may change as the program gets older (it was pretty young still when I attended), but it was the case for me, and I had to make a financial projection for three full years at an expensive university with tuition and high costs of living. There was no way to cut the time down, and failing to finish in three years wasn't an option.

If you don't qualify for the financial aid you need, do the math for what it will cost to live in general and how much you'll need to set aside for school later on. Plenty of parents and guardians want to send their kids to school but can't afford it, leaving them feeling pressured to figure out how to do it anyway. And let me just reiterate here: it's a completely valid option not to go to school, to find a trade school, certification, or some other training, or "DIY" a career path outside of academia. If you're set on going to college but don't have the financial means, it's totally fine to take your time to work out the logistics of financing it. Until college is free for all who seek it, we're stuck trying to do the best can with what we've got.

Doing Some General Math

Let's say you still have no idea what you want to do or whether you want to attend college at all. What are you doing right now? Do you have a part-time job? Can you get one? Can you find tiny ways to make small amounts of money before you've graduated? If you've already graduated, chances are you've made the first step in some direction. So take stock now. Savings + income = what? Once you've figured out what you reasonably have, you'll need to figure out the cost of living in your current and future areas. If you live in a big city like New York or Los Angeles, you already know those are two of the most expensive places to live. If you're not attached to a specific place, perhaps it would be wise to move to a place where the cost of living is drastically smaller, not only so that you have better means to afford it but also so that you can save up more money on the same level of "effort." Do some research and find out the cost of living in several areas you might like. Make sure to include the cost of moving to those places, as well as any upfront costs for a rental (usually the first month's rent and a security deposit, or first and last month's rent plus a deposit). If you're planning on renting, it's important to have at least three months of rent saved up just to cover the moving-in expenses. The upshot of a higher security deposit is that, hopefully, you'll get the whole of it back when you move out. If you are interested in some other living arrangement, you'll still need to figure out the cost of moving into that space. Are you able to stay with a friend or family member for little or no rent? You'll still have expenses. Are you able to stay in a place you've inherited? You'll have taxes, insurance, and maintenance costs. Do you have a dream to live in an RV or motorhome so that you can move your living space around as you see fit? (I actually do this!) You'll need to figure out how much that will cost (and it can cost a lot depending on where you are and what you plan on getting and doing). No matter what this looks like, you need to break down your costs of living for every possibility: the most expensive budget, a middle-ground budget, and a cheap budget. Have all the numbers ready to go before you start trying to decide on schools or other life choices.

CHAPTER 4: ASKING FOR A FRIEND: HOW TO FIND OUT WHAT THE SCHOOL YOU'RE CONSIDERING IS REALLY LIKE

As someone who was super active and engaged with prospective students for my graduate program, I can tell you with full confidence that no one simply showing you around is going to start telling you what it's really like to attend that school. And even if they do, there's no way it can represent what it would be like for *you.*

So, how can you know what it's really like on campus? While there's no guarantee any campus will be exactly like what you are expecting, you can at least figure out some major factors that are consistent for everyone. For instance, even if you aren't interested in Greek life or parties, you'll certainly know whether your school has a reputation for being a "party school." Some schools are highly competitive in a not-so-great way, and you'll notice this even if you aren't actively participating in the rat race. You can do Google searches on "top party schools" and get a broad picture of what some schools on a list made by others are like. You should also Google the schools you're interested in along with "party school" or just "party." This will give you a sense of how seriously the students take studying on the whole. But this is barely the first step.

It'll be a little easier to figure out what life is like for students at the most prestigious schools because there will be more written about them online. For instance, Harvard, Yale, and other Ivy League schools have reputations as top schools in almost every academic field they offer. There will be plenty to read up on regarding housing, the walkability of the campus, etc.

Campus Visits

While I did say it's impossible to know what the experience will be like for you just by visiting, it's important to see a campus in person whenever possible.

There are also probably ways to do a virtual visit if physically traveling to the location is cost prohibitive.

During a campus visit, try to come prepared: Ask questions that are relevant and not open-ended. For example, if you're interested in photography, don't just ask "about the photo lab." Ask about specific capabilities of the lab or any concerns you have about using it: "Does this lab have both black and white and color photo development stations? Will my classes start with black and white, and when will they progress to color?" Back when I was in college and required to take a photography class, there was only a place to develop our black and white film. You could also ask, "How busy does the photo lab get on the weekend?" Depending on the answer, you might need to forgo drinking questionable chemical solutions by dunking your photos in them instead. Or, perhaps you'll find out that everyone floods the photo lab on weekends and that it might be more comfortable to work on Tuesdays at 4 p.m. Therefore, you might want to schedule your classes so as not to interfere with that time slot. Either way, here's the point: Ask questions that will help you work out what the experience might be like *for you* and behaviors and study ethics that *you* already know about yourself. If you're very last minute, don't assume it'll be amazing to have a Monday morning photography class after the photo lab was overflowing on Sunday night when you know you'll be one of those students in there stretching the occupancy limit.

Ask your prospective department for a private

tour. I was very involved in graduate school and often shepherded prospective and newly arriving students around (my graduate program was three years, and I was fielding questions from prospective students by the spring semester of my first year). I never took students across the whole of the campus, and honestly, I wouldn't have been able to address questions or concerns about those things. Graduate students didn't live on campus, in general, so this was a different beast entirely. I was able to take students through where they would actually be learning and into areas they would also have access to with special equipment (my major of Interactive Media covered anything from games to mixed reality or VR). I was also able to answer honestly about our small cohort and the professors for different classes. However, I was also a little bit of a zealot because I firmly believed in leaving the school a better place than when I started. So, while there were some downsides to the program, without the right questions from the students, I would never have just blurted them out. If you do get a tour guide who blurts out how bad things are at the school, you may want to seriously reconsider your interest in that place. Bitterness and resentment are not normal findings on a campus where there are few or no jaded students. It's important to listen to anything negative the students already attending your school of interest have to say.

Even though it was many years ago now, I was pursuing a degree in a creative field and was anxious about competitiveness and intellectual property theft starting way back in high school. Competitiveness, in general, didn't bother me: I could fight any student academically for a top grade with minimal stress but didn't want my creative work to be stolen. This became a significant fear as I had already heard many horror stories before ever setting foot on campus. During tours, I asked any students I could ask about how they interacted with each other and whether they respected each other's creative work. If their answer was cutthroat, I knew I wasn't going to apply to a school that had a high potential for backstabbing and copyright theft. I still applied to about a dozen schools, so mentally striking one off my list based on a bad feeling wasn't going to prevent me from having a sea of options.

Housing

This is another important one to see (or be virtually shown) in person, giving you a decent idea of what kind of space you'll have.

I'm an only child. Until fifth grade, I grew up with my two first cousins living next door during the school year and in the same house when we spent summers together at my grandmother's mobile home. It isn't that I wasn't used to living around people, just around strangers. All these years later, I still consider myself difficult to live with! I feared living in a tiny room with a strange girl. I've had insomnia since age 14 and have a few compulsive habits, so my high school self was internally screaming that having a roommate was *not* going to work. I probably wasn't wrong.

I decided it was worth it to spend extra and roll in the housing lottery to get a single room. I still had to share a bathroom with a floor of girls, which my public bathroom phobia protested, but it was the right choice for me to avoid living with a stranger on top of all the other new stresses of starting college. It wasn't the best time for accommodations, but I probably would fall into a category now that would necessitate my own room and bathroom—which is good news for you!

Since you'll be an incoming freshman, there may be specific dorms for you. There may not be, or you may not be interested in or eligible for, some special programs that have dedicated dorms. If it's a general lottery for housing based on seniority, you may end up living very far from your classes. This was also part of my tradeoff for living alone—I was in the most distant housing from classes, and, even worse, most of my classes were at the opposite ends of the classroom buildings.

Whatever living situations you'll have to pick from, remember that only *you* have control over your actions. When I shared an apartment with roommates in my junior year, I had to keep reminding myself that I couldn't control anyone's behavior in a common area, only mine. I definitely failed to remember that sometimes when I was ready to kick out my messy, obnoxious roommate who was (and still is) one of my closest friends but left dishes in the sink and didn't know how to use a sponge or clean the bathroom. You may get lucky and have no issues whatsoever in your living arrangements for school, but don't expect to face zero conflict in whatever situation you end up choosing.

Competitiveness

I can be quite competitive. However, by the time high school ended, my desire to claw my way to the top had significantly waned. Burnout. I realized there would be competition in whatever program I pursued. I actually avoided applying to a few top schools because they were so deeply entangled with stories of competitiveness, stealing from students (by other students or even professors), and sabotage. The thought of my creative work somehow being stolen was vastly more upsetting than not getting the top grades in the class—which, I'll admit, was upsetting enough. I'm not the only person in the world to take competitiveness at a school or in a specific program into account when charting an academic path.

Now, I won't always be talking so personally in every section of this book, but I will share a little bit more of my story here as an example. I had been worried about copyright troubles—having my work stolen or used or uncredited—since high school. I had heard lots of bad stories starting at a young age about Hollywood and the entertainment industry. So, when I say that I maintained this protectiveness and fear and still do, I want you to know what that means. Guess what? I *still* experienced copyright issues just after I graduated from graduate school. I'm not at liberty to discuss the details, but the point I'm trying to make is that if you fear falling victim to a copyright problem, you can't prevent it all and shouldn't rely on that fantasy to sustain you. The last chapter of my previous book, *The Lazy Student's Guide to Writing Papers and Getting College Done Right: Work Smarter, Not Harder*, talks about doing college (and life) with *integrity*. Living with integrity won't protect you from everything, but it will protect you from a lot. And if you can live with integrity and spread that devotion to others, your peers will likely follow suit, and this *will* soften that competitive anxiety around you.

Let's move on from personal stuff. If you're someone who thrives on and likes competitiveness, then it's understandable that you might want to fight your way into a fantastic program. Everyone is competing to get into every school to some extent, the top programs more so than the community college down the road that will essentially accept you as long as you want to pay and have transcripts proving you have basic high school proficiency. Lots of programs have competition that doesn't end once you're in, though. Are you sure you're ready for this lifestyle? It will be years of intense pressure. If you want to be a doctor, for example—and not just *any* doctor, but a world-renowned surgeon—you'll be competing for many years beyond your application days. You'll compete for top grades to get top residency spots to train with the top surgeons, and so on, for the rest of your life.

The same holds for becoming a top lawyer. You're competing for top grades from day one, and you'll also need to graduate at the top of your class in your elite program to get the most coveted, sought-after legal positions. There's a useful book called *Don't Go to Law School (Unless)* by Paul Campos that I once read to help me to decide whether I wanted to add another advanced degree to my resume. Ultimately, Campos confirmed what I already suspected, and while there was potential (it isn't about persuading you out of law school but a reality check from a law professor with the inside scoop), I was already too deep into the rabbit hole of graduate school and poor health to make such a big commitment. This is exactly what I'm hoping to help you with in this book, for all paths.

CHAPTER 5: AREAS OF STUDY: INTERESTS FOR MAJORS, MINORS, AND GRADUATE TRACKS

There are too many areas of study for me to list them all in this book. Also, that would be kind of ridiculous. However, this chapter *is* about helping you figure out what area(s) of study are suitable for you.

Use the internet!

It feels like an obvious thing to say, but to find information about specific areas of study, career paths, and all sorts of higher education potential, the easiest thing to do is start Googling.

How long is this trip?

Before I break down different paths and areas of study, let's talk about the different kinds of higher education and the degrees that might go along with them.

A **certification** can refer to a completed course at any higher education level. Certification could mean a short course after high school to get certified outside of higher education. Certification could also mean getting certified in a very narrow, specific area beyond a master's degree. The only real rule here is that if you're seeking certification for something, generally, you must have a high school diploma or GED equivalent (an interesting "rule").

Certifications can be good and bad, and I've heard stories that reflect as much from my peers and from my clients. A certification in a technical area like computer networking may be useful, but it may also be in a highly saturated field. A certification might be required to become a plumber or electrician, for instance. A plumber or an electrician might also have some other level of college to attain important credentials, like an associate's degree or a bachelor's degree. Teachers, who often continue their education while teaching to continue up the ladder of seniority, might seek certification in a certain technique or to add a new role to their teaching job. Certifications are neither inherently positive nor negative, and if you ultimately decide to get certified in something, more power to you. There's nothing wrong with enduring a short stint of further education to forge a career path you're satisfied with. In fact, I would encourage you to get a certification for something over taking years and years to graduate with numerous degrees if you're able to pursue that career path without the degree (obviously, if you want to be a doctor, you can't bypass years of medical school).

Licensing is another "type" of higher education that you might need for various reasons. Licensing can be required at any point after your high school equivalent. Licensing is important for many professions, like barbers, plumbers, doctors, and lawyers. Licensing might require very little further education, perhaps equivalent to a certificate, or it may require many years of schooling before being allowed to practice medicine. Licensing might come along with other forms of higher education, like certification or a law degree, but the licensing itself is usually related to passing a test rather than the actual learning.

An **associate's** degree is generally a two-year program offering some basic general education classes and career-path classes. These are flexible degrees, and some states, like Florida, allow you to complete an associate's degree before transferring into a four-year bachelor's program at a state school. This means that you can head to a cheaper community college for the first half of your requirements, then transfer them to a state college or university to finish out your degree at a (still relatively cheap) school with more resources.

The program is supposed to be a "guarantee" to get into your bachelor's program, though stipulations may still apply. Either way, this is a powerful kind of program, especially if you're not certain about the specific track within a major or whether there just isn't the most compatible associate's degree for what you'd like to do.

For example, you might be able to find a veterinary tech track for an associate's degree or a track about animal biology. But what you really want is to become a veterinarian; you just don't have the cash on hand to get into a more expensive bachelor's program right away. Do some research and take advantage of a program like the one I described in Florida. The idea is to get as many general credits as you can toward your major after you've transferred and transitioned into your bachelor's program, where (presumably) you'll have much better access to hands-on and more specialized classes and experiences than at the community college.

There are plenty of career paths that require an associate's degree alone. A quick Google search reveals that most plumbers, for example, have a certification or associate's degree only in plumbing. An associate's degree might also be handy to give you an edge in many other career tracks, especially if you're unsure of what you want to do. If you're happy to be an entry-level assistant at a law firm for a few years before deciding whether you truly want to go to law school, an associate's degree might come in handy for you or may simply be a way to slowly get general requirements for inevitably heading off to more schooling. If you end up not liking that career path after a year or two and are content with the associate's degree, you'll have an easy time pivoting onto a different track or using the associate's degree to get a lot of general requirements completed before heading into a bachelor's program. Two years is nothing to sneeze at, but it's a more compact amount of higher education and can be a great option for many situations.

A **bachelor's degree** is generally earned from a four-year college or university. In just about all scenarios, if you're on a career path for something that requires a master's degree or a special law or medical degree, you're going to need a bachelor's degree first. Most bachelor's degrees consist of 60 credits of general requirements and 60 credits of specific requirements for the major. I hate this phrase, but "back in my day," I was very lucky that my undergraduate institution had very few general requirements, leaving me free to pick from a huge pool of classes. I know some people were thrilled about all the majors my school offered because it meant they had no math requirements. I was happy to take many different classes, but it was nice that I wasn't required to take any advanced science classes (I feared them after, sadly, not having a lot of science teachers to learn throughout my primary education). I'd have happily taken certain science classes, though I never managed to get an open seat in the few I was interested in. The great part about my major was that I got to pick classes at will. If I wasn't too interested in a subject, I never had to continue it. This is precisely what happened when I took an anthropology class and *hated it* by halfway through. I was able to take a class about disability culture instead and pretty much every sociology and legal studies class I could fit into my schedule. If you're headed into something that requires further education beyond your bachelor's degree, I'd highly recommend finding the broadest program you can to spread your interests around. I would definitely not recommend sacrificing your favorite school or the "top schools" for certain things, though, in lieu of finding the broadest program possible. Of course, if you're heading to Harvard or Yale on a full scholarship and have your heart set on law school, don't worry about the flexibility of the major—just go!

A bachelor's degree has a few common iterations:

* Bachelor of Arts (BA)
* Bachelor of Science (BS)
* Bachelor of Fine Arts (BFA)
* Bachelor of Applied Science (BAS)
* Bachelor of Engineering (BE)

I can't very well explain every point of difference because I'd prefer to get this book in your hands before the end of time. I'm going to generalize about what each of these means for two reasons: 1) the differences only really matter in relation to whether or not the program provides what you're looking for, and 2) for most undergraduate students, the specific letter soup involved in your bachelor's degree will be meaningless in relation to your career path.

A Bachelor of Arts (BA) degree tends to be for liberal arts, humanities, and social sciences. This is one of the most common degrees that people receive. Don't let the word "arts" fool you into thinking this must be a creative degree. It's just the remnant of a bygone age when the term was more inclusive. A Bachelor of Science degree will tend to be for more technical disciplines, which can include creative and artistic disciplines like film and photography. A Bachelor of Fine Arts degree generally covers an analytical focus on the liberal arts. This could mean a film degree focusing on analysis rather than production. A Bachelor of Applied Science degree is more like it sounds, tending to be a hands-on scientific or technical degree. A Bachelor of Engineering is generally an engineering degree without as broad a range as the others.

Again, to be clear, you have hardly any reason to care about the name of the degree in most situations. My undergraduate degree was a Bachelor of Science in Cinema and Photography with a concentration in Screenwriting. There was also a Bachelor of Arts and Bachelor of Fine Arts degree involving film at the same time. As I said, it's much more important that you pick the degree that will give you the experiences you're looking for.

Each college or university will also be broken into schools. For example, my undergraduate degree was in the School of Communications and included all of those degrees I previously mentioned. The school itself had different requirements than other schools on campus, including (and a big reason many of my classmates chose their paths as they did) no science or math requirements. I didn't go there because of that since I really liked math, but I *did* appreciate that I had huge freedom to take any classes I wanted to make up most of the credit requirements with very few specific course requirements. When you're looking at a degree at a particular college, you'll want to investigate the school in which the degree is housed for this reason more than you need to care about the type of degree that has been assigned to the major.

A **master's** degree can be categorized in two ways: 1) as a "terminal" degree, meaning there really isn't much of a need for further education (or, perhaps, there simply isn't any higher degree out there that exists), and 2) as a form of mastery that may sometimes be leveraged into an even higher-level degree. As the name implies, when you're done with any degree of this type, you'll be a "master" of this subject. A master's degree is indicative of highly specialized learning and will require a completed bachelor's degree.

Most master's degrees require one to two years of full-time study. There are always outliers, however, such as my master's, which was three full years of study. Mine was a terminal degree, meaning there was no need for further degrees in that field. Some master's degree programs are bundled into your bachelor's degree as a "fifth-year" program through a school; others will be bridges into a different, higher degree like a Ph.D., where you officially receive the master's degree related to the many years of study to complete the Ph.D. along with the Ph.D. itself. Master's degrees that are an extra year on top of your bachelor's degree are called integrated master's degrees. Not much about these terms is important except that each program will have pros and cons for your goals and needs. For example, an integrated degree might be really helpful if you want to pursue a specific sort of engineering for which you likely need a master's degree to qualify but getting started to work is very important to you. You'll have the advanced credentials needed in less time (which also means fewer student loans on your back).

A **doctoral degree** or Ph.D. is a highly advanced degree involving numerous years in research and practice of your craft. Doctoral degrees cover the sciences, including psychology, medicine, philosophy, engineering, and so on. Simply pursuing a Ph.D. for the sake of it would be a huge and unnecessary undertaking. Many doctoral students (as they're called) are pursuing a career in research and teaching, though not all such degrees lead to a life of academia, as in our medical research example.

There are plenty of specialized doctoral degrees, but since this book is about figuring out a plan for your future, I'm going to keep this part as simple as I can. You may earn a doctoral or master's degree as part of going through law school. You may earn an M.D. or D.O.

to practice medicine. You may earn a Ph.D., as I said, in a large list of fields, some of which will inevitably lead to teaching and/or research, while others will guide you toward your specific field (some psychologists and therapists won't become medical doctors but will need a Ph.D. for their licensing, for instance). If you have a career track in mind that requires an advanced degree, your research into schools and programs will illuminate the best doctoral degree path for you.

One Last "Degree" to Talk About

Being educated is great, but I think that it also closely correlates with actually wanting to go through all the hoops involved in receiving any credentials. There are plenty of other paths.

I have a friend who I met in college and (happily) is still one of my closest friends. He started selling items online while he was still in high school. His degree wasn't in business. He's now long since paid off his student loans, has a storefront, has around a dozen employees or more at any given time, and his business is still thriving even through the uncertainty and closing caused by the COVID-19 pandemic. I know he's grateful for the life experience, but he's never had any need of that degree in working for *himself* all these years.

I know of several self-employed, successful people who started out with nothing or with a small, smart investment of money, service, or time.

While there are many "self-made" people who were more "lucky and rich already" than self-made, there are plenty of "social influencers," content makers (YouTube, Twitch), and small startups that have found solutions to problems and provided a service or product that grew their business many times over. Some people learn outside of the higher education system how to be great investors, amazing salespeople, or incredible storytellers. There are many "career paths" I certainly can't just come up with off the top of my head, too, and new careers will arise in the future that I cannot predict, just as my grandparents could never have predicted the existence of cryptocurrency. The only thing I *can* predict with certainty is that unfathomable changes are inevitable. For those who are of the spirit to keep their eyes open to opportunities, that's a good thing.

CHAPTER 6: PUBLIC OR PRIVATE COLLEGE OR UNIVERSITY: WHAT MATTERS FOR WHAT YOU'RE INTERESTED IN DOING?

In general, I wouldn't advise anybody to go to a private (usually more expensive) college or university *unless*:

* the program you are interested in is highly specific and unique

* you want to get into a top law school because

you have plans to become a lawyer (graduating from any law school will leave you in a saturated market versus being from the top schools and having the right connections)

* your job is offering to pay for tuition for a specific degree or program somewhere

* you're headed to medical school, and undergraduates are heavily favored by the school (only consider this a valid reason if it's *verifiably and statistically true*)

* you qualify for a full ride, whether through financial aid and grants or a scholarship—obviously, go to the best, most suitable place you can

If your parent(s) or grandparent(s) or other close relatives have attended or are currently attending a school, sometimes this will be considered when determining your acceptance and/or scholarships. If nepotism can benefit you to earn a degree you actually want, then there's no reason not to leverage it. Both of my parents earned degrees at the nearby (good) university. It was a valid option. Some of my high school classmates were headed there. My grandmother went there before it was a university. I was an excellent student and was offered scholarships from other schools, too, but this school was within walking distance from the house I grew up in. The scholarship would've covered room and board if I wanted to go there, too. However, I didn't want to go to school minutes away from my parents (which is a super bonus for some people, I know), and I didn't feel that it was a particularly strong program for what I was interested in. So, I didn't go. I'm sharing this because 1) I was easily accepted via an early/immediate decision based on my high school record and family's history at the school, and 2) they offered me a big scholarship practically in the same breath as "Oh, did your parents meet on campus?" (In fact, they met years after they'd graduated.)

Having relatives who earned a degree at the same school isn't only about nepotism. Schools also take pride in generational academic achievement because it highlights their legacies. Sure, some of the motivation is because families with a long line of graduates from, say, an Ivy League school are more likely to be wealthy enough to pay the high price tag of attendance, but there is also some validity to accepting new students of successfully graduated relatives.

All of that said, no matter what your financial budget or target school or program, you should spend your time filling out applications *and* all the scholarships and grants you can find. A $500 grant when your goal is to attend a $50,000-a-year school may seem pointless, but prior to acceptance to both the school or winning those scholarships and grants, you never know how useful that $500 might be. Five Benjamins is a stash of rented or used books; it's two months of food; it's a plane, train, or bus ticket to visit your hometown; it's a chunk of a top-of-the-line computer or a nicely priced tablet. It may seem unrealistic to seek out 100 tiny scholarships or grants, and it's pretty unlikely that you can fully fund an expensive school this way, but if you get even one small award like this, well...it's better than not having it at all.

When to Pivot

If you've read this far, you'll see I'm pretty opposed to diving into expensive places without a solid plan. Sure, it's no fun putting yourself into debt or sending yourself to a place you don't like or enjoy. It's also a sign of misunderstanding when students do this. The school's name does carry some weight, but it's not *that* important in the *vast majority* of circumstances you'll encounter beyond graduation.

I've already said it, and I'll continue to emphasize it: Community colleges for learning the required skills and experience and earning the qualifications you need for what you want to do are amazing. They don't put you into crippling debt. You can even spend some years at a community college and transfer to get that fancy prestigious name on your diploma if that's still important to you or if the program is special enough to warrant the transfer. Getting general education requirements from your local community college is a great way to accelerate your time in the expensive school as well—you can even start taking classes while completing your high school degree. This will shave off some time from the more expensive school. Most high schools offer AP classes, but even if yours doesn't, *you can still sign up to take the AP test and study for yourself.*

Upon entering college, I was able to receive credit for my passing AP scores toward my degree, along with two courses that I attended in my senior year at (you guessed it) the university within walking distance from my house. I left school at around 11:30 every day to attend my college course *once a week* in the afternoon. Had I been more ambitious, I could've taken a second class or managed to accrue more AP credits (I did *not* pass the AP history test, and I regretted not signing up for the AP calculus test that I probably would have passed since math always came easily to me and my calculus class covered most of what would have been on the test anyway).

If you've ever wanted to attend an expensive school, it's time to think about that right now. Wasted time won't ever come back. It's a waste of time if you get through four years at any school and realize you still need three credits to graduate, meaning you'll have *yet another* semester of fees to finish. It's a waste of time (and possibly money) to head to Harvard to take English 101 when you're majoring in biology. Why can't those credits be racked up with less pressure and less financial and time investment? Maybe your local community college English 101 class is going to be less intensive than at Harvard, but your professors will be especially eager to help their students pass and do well. Community colleges want to build their reputations and prove their legacies just as much as (if not more than) those private, established, and expensive schools.

I want you to abandon any beliefs you're clinging

to about "how it's supposed to be" after having read this chapter. There's no reason to tie yourself to any path simply because that's what you think you're "supposed" to do. Drop any toxic idea you have about what to do when you graduate. Don't stretch yourself thin without the clearest of goals. Don't head off to an expensive school just because someone else thinks it's good for you or with vague ideas of what you might do with a special, unique, or elite degree. You'll feel the effects of that far more than it's worth.

CHAPTER 7: APPLICATIONS: HOW TO DECIDE WHICH SCHOOLS TO ACTUALLY APPLY FOR

There are a few strategies for applying to schools across different situations. The best-known approach is to apply to a few "backup schools" with decent programs and at least one "dream school" that you really want to attend, regardless of your chances. This isn't a terrible strategy by any means, but it can amount to a lot of nail biting until you get all your decisions back!

Before you start applying, you've likely, as outlined in this book's previous chapters, checked out all the different programs and price ranges for schools that match your educational needs. One thing to keep in mind is that even if you apply to numerous "safety" or "backup" schools and don't get in, you are almost certainly able to attend a local community college. If you can pay the (generally nominal) tuition fees, you can attend. You'll probably need your GED or high school diploma and to submit some forms, but the process is mostly painless. *This* is your backup. First, it will alleviate some of the anxiety that can easily turn into paranoia ("I won't get into any schools, and my life will be over!!"). Second, you might get into that dream school and no others and be unfortunate enough that you don't get any financial aid or scholarship money. And even if it's the school you'd prefer, unless it's one of those very, very special circumstances I discussed previously, you probably should be flexible enough to alter your plans. Go to the cheaper school, bang out some credits, reapply, and look for scholarships and financial aid again. Work part-time. Work full-time if you can manage it. Either way, don't get caught up in the words "safety" and "dream" when applying to schools. You'll get lost quickly in the muddy waters of stress and anxiety.

That said, you probably want to try applying to as many schools as you can reasonably afford. Some high schools can help you with programs that require only one fee for applications and allow you to apply to as many as you want (under a certain cap). I don't have experience with those, but if it's free/cheap, apply to every school you might possibly want to attend. Some schools will also waive their application fees, and you should apply to any and all schools you have an interest in that will let you apply for free.

While the maximum number of schools you should apply to depends on your personal goals, keep in mind that nobody needs to apply to fifty schools. I applied to a lot of undergraduate schools at the behest of my parents, but I applied to a single graduate school because it had the exact program I wanted and was highly specialized. Applying elsewhere simply had no value for me. Don't apply to schools you have no interest in attending. If you're unsure of what major you'd like to pursue but are debating between two that are good, solid programs at a single school you really like, this takes huge pressure off.

There are a few options aside from the standard application process to look into. Early Decision and Immediate Decision Days are two solid examples. Plenty of schools offer Early Decision, which involves an expedited application and decision process. It's basically how it sounds. The tradeoff of these decisions may be that you must decide whether you are attending or not sooner than if you had applied the regular way. Early Decision at a school you really want to go to may be a practical way to set your goals in motion quickly, though. Immediate Decision Days are also what they sound like: a day or several days dedicated to presenting your application and getting an acceptance or rejection on the spot. You probably don't need to decide to accept the offer that day, but you may have to decide a little sooner than if you went through the standard process.

Both of these are sound options if you know exactly what you want to do or have one or two schools firmly on your radar. If you know where you want to go and what your plans are, you may realize while starting the application process that it's a lot of time waiting for answers otherwise. If the school you want has an Immediate Decision Day in October of your senior year and you get accepted, you'll have an incentive to figure out all the financial plans and continue working to find more scholarships and grant money. If you have several desired schools and they all offer early or immediate decisions, you'll be able to work out your plans well before those last months of senior year when everybody is anxious but *over* doing any more work.

Overall, you should have a good sense of what you want to do before you start sending applications anywhere. This will save you a lot of headaches and wasted time. Even if the school seems way out of your league but you know it's ideal, apply anyway. Don't give up before trying. I've heard from many people who regret spending so much time wishing that there had been an opportunity or that they had taken chances that they were afraid to take. If your family or friends—or, hell, even your *goldfish*—puts pressure on you about what to do or what not to do, you must summon the strength to ignore this. *Your life* will be affected by these choices, *not theirs.* Having goals that match your needs and desires in life is *never* selfish.

Plan a good amount of time to sit down and

make a list of suitable schools. Set an application budget. Work out exactly what will best fit your needs as you currently see them. Remember that your task is to plan an efficient path to reach your goals but that your goals may change as you proceed. Allow yourself to feel enough pressure to remain motivated while keeping feelings of overwhelm at bay by sticking to the parameters and plans you're setting up in advance. Once you decide to apply to a school, move through the process in a "black and white" way and don't let anxieties and doubts derail you. Filling out applications can be time-consuming, and you may find that it demands more of your effort than you think it will before getting started.

Requirements

Once you've figured out which programs you want to apply to, don't forget to sign up for and/or take the testing required for the applications to each program. You're almost certainly going to need SAT or ACT scores at the bare minimum unless you're going to community college or some other type of program, such as a trade school, as previously discussed in this book. You may need to take other tests as well. If you're trying to get into a foreign school, for example, keep an eye out for any language testing requirements.

Depending on what program you're going into, you may need to take other entrance exams. If you're already taking (or looking to take) AP classes in your junior and senior year of high school, you'll want to figure out what scores are required to receive credit for those classes toward your college degree as determined by your program's policies.

Once registered in a school, you'll likely be required to take placement tests there, too. Leading up to the first semester, all incoming freshmen at my college had to take a math placement test and a writing placement test. The school itself had requirements in place, and these tests were the only opportunities to test out of those requirements.

CHAPTER 8: PERSONAL ESSAYS: HOW TO WRITE THE BEST PERSONAL STATEMENTS AND APPLICATION MATERIAL POSSIBLE

I'm going to let you in on the dark secret of personal essays: They're not as terrible as they seem. No, really. They're great application tools if you do them right. They can also be the bane of your existence if you're not careful.

In my freelancing, I've had a number of clients who are seeking editing/writing for their personal essays for applications. Unlike with clients who try to get me to do their homework, I sometimes get very involved in crafting these essays. Let me explain how the process works from the standpoint of an experienced editor before I offer some writing tips.

When a (potential) client requests assistance with their application essays, after agreeing to the gig, I immediately work to get to know them a little. I read the application material over and check out the school's website for the program they are applying to. I had a lovely repeat client who one day asked me to work with her on her essay to apply to transfer schools. I already knew her writing style and a little bit about her by then, but she sent me a long essay needing paring down and edits for flow and content. She'd written a really interesting and moving essay already, so my job was to ensure it met the maximum character limit, read well, and felt genuine. I spent most of my time focusing on her reasoning for entering the program to prevent her essay from sounding stilted and dry. Going from an intimate look into one's life to "I want to learn at your school because it's a good school" is jarring and comes across as disinterest. When I'm editing, I want to ensure that a personal essay relates motivations for attending the school without fawning or including vagaries that immediately bore the reader.

Don't. Write. This.

Some clients think their personal essays need to endlessly praise the school or take an approach that, ultimately, comes across as entitled. They discuss at length how they really want to go to a prestigious school. This is a terrible idea for a variety of reasons. One, it only highlights entitlement from you as a potential student by saying that your interest in this school is all about names and labels, not what the school can provide for your field, the prestige *you* can bring to the school, or what's actually great about the school itself. Two, it says nothing valuable about yourself. Three, it still doesn't prove you know anything about the school or have done any research or soul searching about your goals in life and the paths that might help you achieve them.

When clients come to me with a mottled outline or an essay draft that lacks substance, my priority is to learn more about who they are. Instead of that stiff sentiment of "I want to go to your school," putting in real meat about yourself in relation to the school and program you're applying to makes your application stand out.

Some applicants approach these essays with dread, and it comes out clearly in their drafts. If you're fearful about lacking the qualifications or extracurricular activities or harbor some other anxiety related to being accepted, you can bet it will show in your writing. I've had clients who end up with paragraphs of apologetic lists of how they've been lacking in whatever quality supported by ambitious yet vague promises to do better. This is a huge turnoff. It's also tedious. You don't want the people reading your application essays to be so disinterested that they immediately forget about your application, but making the above mistakes is a surefire way to accomplish exactly that.

Your perceived lack of something you're apologizing for reads like an attempt at pity or a list of excuses. You might not even be lacking in some quality the school is looking for, but pointing it out and being ashamed about it and/or promising some change will create a perceived deficit in you for the reader. Some schools receive countless applications, and the people reading your essays are human, too. It's easy to get lost in the shuffle. You don't want to increase your chances of such misfortune by giving the reader a reason to *stop reading and put your application into the rejection pile*. I care about helping my clients very deeply and take pride in doing a good job for them, but I can generally tell what's a good piece of writing and what will need a rewrite and a lot more work within the first two paragraphs, if not the first two sentences. If reading application essays was my job, I'd probably read a bad essay in its entirety as a courtesy while already knowing it was worthy of rejection. I have no doubts that admissions officers feel this way.

I've seen another approach to essay writing that revolves around listing off accomplishments in a way that can only be read as a brag (or, at best, a "humblebrag," which is no different). For example, I had a client whose son was trying to get into an exclusive high school program. He was helping his son draft something for me to edit, so both of them sent several drafts of multiple essays that were little more than lists in paragraph form. The young man was clearly very smart, talented, and actively learning many things. While it was good to represent his efforts in the essays, it took several drafts to present his interests and areas of self-study without listing off his many credentials out of context.

In helping this client, I immediately noticed another common mistake as I worked to guide the essays to be about the teenager's life as a whole. He had a passion for many science and engineering fields and was trying to articulate how he wanted to merge those interests to pursue life goals, which was great, but it took several drafts to remove all the "I want to go here because it will open doors to a great life." While it isn't untrue that getting into the program of your dreams will be helpful in achieving your goals, this sentiment completely removes the acknowledgment of experience and maturity in growing as a person to achieve them. The school he applied to accepted similarly brilliant students with similar lists of extracurriculars and interests. *All* those students had some qualifications like competition wins or achievement tests under their belts. Instead, it was important to guide the reader of their essays in understanding how those great things helped the applicants become better as people in some way. You want your reader to understand you as an individual and see what sets you apart from the crowd and makes you an asset worth pursuing. You also want the reader to believe, whether or not you are accepted and attend their school/program, that you are a capable individual who won't let a rejection stand in the way of your integrity, empathy, and motivations. This makes you an incredibly appealing candidate and sets you up for acceptance.

Planning Your Essay

Many applications will request a response of varying length to their questions, but the purpose of these questions is to demonstrate who you are and why you want to attend their school and program. They already know you want to go there because it's a good school, or *you wouldn't spend your time, energy, and possibly money on applying there.* They don't need you to tell them about their school or program, either. They know what the school offers. They want to know how you fit into that.

Let's take a brief trip into the process of entering higher education over the past hundred or so years. I mentioned earlier that my grandmother had gone to the local university before it was a university. Before her death, she was the oldest living alum for quite a while. My grandmother was a teacher who was even asked by the principal to step in and substitute for younger grades while she was still in high school. It was clear she would become a teacher. She was good at it, she liked it, and, having been born in 1910 to a family with numerous older siblings and living through world wars and national depressions, she wanted to earn the best living she could. They needed teachers, and she needed qualifications, so she finished, got her high school diploma, and went to the nearby school to pursue higher education. I cannot recall what degree she acquired, but it was enough to start teaching immediately. She continued to teach through schools unable to pay their teachers properly, through the baby boom and raising her own children, through her husband's early passing, and even after her retirement, tutoring children in her home past the age of 100. She only really stopped when clients from the local schools dwindled.

In addition to being an excellent teacher, my grandmother was a great example of how education requirements have both changed and stayed the same. She fulfilled her teaching requirements and pursued her goals. That part of a higher education path remains the same: you find the requirements you need while keeping up with new or changing information and qualifications. My grandmother had tried and true methods for teaching, but she also continued to learn what was changing in the wide field of education to adapt to it. Children would bring along their homework, and my grandmother had to teach them whatever was in their textbooks to help them complete it. On the other hand, her experience is less relevant now. Yes, the point of higher education remains the same, but there are vastly more incoming students and competition, the perceived need for degrees has significantly increased, tuition has skyrocketed, and there's now an attitude that everyone must attend some form of higher education if they want to achieve value as a person.

Requirements for teachers were hardly standardized in the late 20s and early 30s when my grandmother was getting started, yet my peers born in the 80s who became teachers graduated high school *expecting* that they would need to continue their education beyond a bachelor's degree. My mother, born in 1950, spent some years of my childhood and early teenage years accruing more credits on top of a master's degree to climb the pay scale. It may seem like I'm only talking about teaching, and maybe it doesn't mean anything to you, but this is how all of academia has expanded to affect careers. Pursuing higher education used to be vastly less necessary to pursue many careers. The word "scholar" was more relevant and referred to a student who continued through many years of higher education in pursuit of knowledge beyond the required qualifications. Academics pursued research for the sake of research. Now, academics are much more pressured. The world of academia is less of a privilege and more of a requirement to accomplish goals in life. This also results in many students who would not have wanted to attend college were they born a hundred years earlier or would simply have had no reason to.

What does all of this have to do with writing your essay? I want you to start planning your application essays with some perspective. If you're currently at that point in the process, then you've already set your sights on a school/program/training program and wrestled with figuring out your needs to get there. I'm not trying to make you doubt your choices; I just want you to write in a calm, collected frame of mind to produce memorable answers to the essay questions.

Let's say I'm applying to the School of Amazing Essayists (yes, I'm making stuff up), and the question on the application reads as follows:

Describe a time in your life when you encountered an obstacle and how you dealt with it. Limit your response to 600 words.

You might be groaning aloud already—and, believe me, I'm with you—but these questions actually give you plenty of opportunities to shine. Here's my "first draft" for this essay.

I had a lot of experience helping other students in working out college paths, editing their papers and even applications to college, and tutoring to help improve their writing experience. I have been freelancing for over a decade, and most of my clients were students who clearly needed more information about how to write a solid research paper. I genuinely enjoy helping others and passing along my knowledge and experience, so I was trying to figure out ways to supplement my effect on the world beyond the simple one-on-one gig work I was already doing.

In 2020, prior to the pandemic, I was complaining to friends and family about how I wanted to do more freelance work as I was experiencing a natural dip in academic clients (a lot of my work relies on word of mouth or repeat clients, and another batch was finishing up school). I have often complained that, each year, students seem to be less prepared for college and have a poorer grasp of writing than ever. In February of that same year, someone asked me, "Why don't you write a book about this?" At first, it seemed silly: My core work, not my freelance work that I consider a "side hustle," is original fiction across many media platforms. But I wanted to put what I consider important information into the world.

Only a few days into starting the book, the pandemic hit, which slowed my other freelance work down significantly. I now had extra time for my media production company but still needed the supplemental income from the freelance work. I debated for a couple of weeks about finishing the book while I started to acquire some new freelance clients and work to maintain my estimated annual income (this is how I keep my health insurance). Finally, after I lined up more freelance work to compensate for the initial drop during the pandemic, I got back to work in full swing. I finished the first draft about a week and a half after that. I then had the book edited and recorded the entire audiobook myself (paying a friend to edit the audio), designed the cover and inside layout myself, and managed to publish the book through my company on Amazon. I had written books before, but all of them are unpublished fiction, so it was especially useful to experience the process of copyrighting a book (I've copyrighted other media) and assigning an ISBN number to it.

I could have succumbed to any of these obstacles along the way. I am also chronically ill and experience many days in any given week, month, or year overwhelmed by pain, vertigo, or fatigue. While these things did and do delay some of my progress, publishing the book is a fantastic reminder that even if it's a little slow going, giving up is a tragic waste. I hope my book continues to help students for years to come. It was so inspiring to write that I am now writing a second (and a third) book aimed at students.

The above essay comes in at 510 words. It's not the most dramatic obstacle, but I stand behind its validity. You want to structure essays like this around honest self-reflection. Mine isn't spectacularly personal, but it's a true and honest portrayal of why I started writing this series of nonfiction books (the book you're reading now is the second one mentioned in the essay).

Honest self-reflection is the takeaway here. You'll want to set aside enough time to express it in writing properly. You might have application essays that aren't very similar. Start by gathering every question you need to answer and creating outlines for them. You can organize these thoughts however works best for you, but I'm going to describe how I would go about it. I would take each question and put them into a document, then consider which are similar and which are not. Similar questions will get similar answers with slight tailoring to each application (perhaps two applications call for reflection on an obstacle you faced, but one is 1000 words maximum while the other is 300, or one asks you to discuss an obstacle related to a specific subject) so they can all have the same outline.

For each question, whether it's about an obstacle or something else, consider how you *really* feel about the question. The question in my hypothetical example isn't meant to determine who has experienced the hardest obstacles; it's about discovering how *you as an individual* have learned to cope and deal with obstacles. Some obstacles you could write about might have positive outcomes. If, for example, you had some terrible accident and lost a limb or limbs (not that I would ever wish that upon anyone), the outcome of that obstacle and how you deal with it won't be that you regrew a limb but, rather, how you learned to cope and continue on through life. It doesn't mean you must be overly upbeat about anything, either. Admissions officers aren't going to be impressed by toxic positivity or platitudes.

Such questions evaluate your ability to be flexible, keep your motivations in focus in spite of problems that can and will arise, and deal with success and failure in equal measure. This is why I said my example isn't fancy or spectacular. I merely offered a broader anecdote simply to demonstrate the writing approach. Your outline should include:

* *A clear obstacle/problem.* In my example, the obstacle is wanting to relay my experience and knowledge to more people.

Why is this an obstacle for you, and why does it matter? In my example, I discuss that I value helping others in improving their writing and reducing the stress around it.

How did you overcome or cope with this obstacle? What rationale did you apply to either use the obstacle to your advantage or find ways to cope with it if the goal was not to overcome it? For my example, the answer was simply to write a book and try not to pressure myself too much when it got delayed.

The results. In my case, that was publishing the book and learning some more about publishing books

How the results affected your life and/or the lives of others. For me, it was a genuine hope that my book would help readers for years to come.

This kind of self-reflection is necessary for any questions you may come across. If you must answer questions about why you want to go to a specific school, answer that honestly as well. Some tips on what to touch on in such an essay:

* What your interests are on the whole.

* Your current plan for the next few years of your life. It's okay if this is a tentative plan or if there is almost no plan at all! If you're fuzzy on what your plan is, include what you do know and why you're still working to figure out what you want to do beyond that. For example, if you are applying to a General Studies program until you can decide between a biology, writing, and business major, but all of those programs

are excellent at the school you are applying to, be sure to describe this quandary.

* When applying to a specific program or school within the college system, mention the positive things they have there but *keep it relevant.* If you're going to major in photography, then speaking about how excited you'd be to have access to that fantastic photo lab is good, but don't extol the wonders of the school's biology lab in that case.

* Don't go overboard with namedropping. Sure, you want to go to this program for good reasons. Don't make it sound like you Googled the school and are just parroting back "your school is good" in this essay. If you mention a positive trait within the school or program or even a professor, do so with a clear purpose.

* Discuss your thoughts on how you will be an excellent student in this program. Use the specifics you've already touched on to enhance these points. If you're interested in photography and have already said as much, tie this in with how you have some specific ideas in mind for the work or research you would do at this school. Perhaps you want to use their resources to create a lenticular image (a type of freely viewable 3D image printed on a 2D canvas), which would definitely be different than a generic answer about wanting to be the next Ansel Adams. Show the admissions officers that you have ambition and are interested in pursuits that will bring prestige to the school while you are there and after you have graduated.

* Find ways to highlight your passions and motivations that you are *already* doing every day. If you want to pursue robotics in college, talk about what you already do every day when thinking and learning about robotics, starting from when you wake up each morning. My undergraduate essays, for example, referenced a long story I'd been writing from middle school through the middle of high school and how my desire to make that story into a movie or series continued motivating me to write more stories and consume not only movies or books, but games as well. Don't *make up* what your life is like; be honest, or you may end up writing what you think they want to hear and discovering you were totally wrong.

After all this soul searching and writing, make sure you have *someone else* edit the essay(s) for you. Many of my freelance gigs solely involve editing and improving essays like these. If you can't afford to hire someone, ask a teacher, librarian, or another adult with experience in college essays (in other words, someone who must have done this at least for themselves before). If you must, swap essays with your classmates and try to hone everyone's essays until they all read professionally but honestly. As a note for an editor's average rates for such a project: I would likely never take a job like this for $20 or less, but depending on the length and the level at which I am familiar with the client, I would probably take an editing gig for a short essay or two (under 1500 words) from a repeat client for $25-$40 (one of my biggest repeat customers, who graduated a few years back, could have asked me to edit a 600-word essay, and I might have charged her only $2 because working on any of her writing barely ever took me any time after years of working with her). New clients will likely encounter higher rates, particularly if the essay is in an incomplete state or needs to be especially long, and editors like me will hear your needs and decide on a flat rate or hourly rate. These projects shouldn't take a skillful editor more than an hour or two.

CHAPTER 9: MANAGING EXPECTATIONS: WHAT TO DO WHILE WAITING FOR ANSWERS

You've sent in all the required application materials. Yay! It's probably all you can think about, so what are you supposed to do once you have no control over what happens next?

Nothing. Doing nothing for a little while is crucial. Enjoy your prom. Head to the movies with friends. Take a nap. Don't start skipping school or letting your grades drop, but do let yourself experience calm for a little while. There isn't anything you can do about those applications now that they've been mailed off or submitted online. And you don't want to do anything about them now anyway—admissions officers aren't going to be on your side if you call or email them out of nerves.

Once you've done your "nothing" for a while, the serious answer to what's next comes into play. You'll undoubtedly have a window of time in which you receive an influx of news regarding acceptance or rejection. If you're feeling especially anxious about this ("What if I'm rejected by all 32,377,983,442 of the schools I applied to?!"), it might help to try to think logically about what you will do in the unlikely event that your preferred future plans don't come to fruition. Unless you don't have a GED or are currently dealing with extreme problems in life, such as a death in the family, homelessness, addiction, or abuse, you're always going to be able to find a community college or some online accredited college to match your basic needs no matter what your future plans are (doctors and lawyers and everything in between can start out in community colleges and be successful even if the original goal was to go Ivy League all the way). If your future plans feel like they would be too tainted if every letter you receive is a rejection, do some more soul searching into what you might prefer to do. Might you head into the military and leverage the assistance of active duty and veteran programs to help you follow that original path at some point in the future? Would a "gap year" of travel help clear your head? Would trying to start some other career path set you up for a different life path that you would find satisfying? Would simply working whatever job you can and saving up feel like a safe path?

The chances are that you're going to get into at least one of your choices. Remember, though, that if you don't get into that coveted program or school, you can try again next year. You also should remind yourself that because the most popular schools have many thousands more applicants than admissions officers, you should never take it personally if your application didn't end up in the acceptance pile. I've seen plenty of accounts in which admissions staff lament their inability to accept every qualified student. Should you end up being rejected from the school you *really* wanted to attend, it's reasonable to build connections with the admissions officers, program directors, and students/alumni from that degree program over the next year. Ask them questions about how you can reapply, what your chances might be, and what the program is looking for in new students. You might realize that you're interested in shifting focus to something you didn't highlight or didn't know yet. If you are respectful and thankful when you ask questions like you would have been prior to applying, this might be helpful in putting your name into the heads of the admissions officers. They will see you as being so interested in their school that you're willing to learn more and reapply because you have a genuine passion.

All in all, I'm not trying to give you more "homework" for crafting a plan as much as convey how managing your expectations can help reduce the

"What am I doing with my life?" anxiety that affects most people at this point in the process. Whether you get into every school you applied to and will soon need to make a decision about where to attend or you need to completely rework your life plan, don't forget: *While you are waiting, you have no control over any of this.* And you didn't have full control over the whole process prior to submission, either. You can control what you write and send in, your grades, and scores, but you can't control what will happen once everything is submitted. You can't control what number in line your application will be or which officer might spill coffee all over yours and be more likely to shunt it aside into whichever pile it falls into. You can't control how many other applicants are your competition this year. Humans like to feel in control, but taking some amount of time, without making excuses for yourself in all things, to acknowledge that you are only able to do your best can be quite useful in mitigating anxiety and managing your expectations. You did a lot of work and put in a lot of effort to get to this point, but so did many others, and the fact that you worked hard has no effect on many of the factors involved in the outcome.

CHAPTER 10: SCHOLARSHIPS/ GRANTS/ FINANCIAL AID: HOW TO FIND AND APPLY TO THE MOST HELPFUL SOURCES OF MONEY FOR YOU

You got into the school of your dreams! Oh…now what *again*?? It's easy to let your excitement over that acceptance letter distract you from the fact that you might still need to keep looking for financial aid. You'll likely have already filled out your FAFSA or known about it and gotten started by now. You've also probably applied to plenty of scholarships, grants, and financial aid. But, until now, even if you won them, you didn't know where that money was going specifically. After you've celebrated a bit, set aside some time to go over your finances with the school, look over any financial aid packages or scholarships you may have been awarded along with your acceptance letter, and figure out your tentative academic budget.

If you find you still want/need more money (or any money) for school, there's still time to keep searching. I'm also hoping you'll skip to this chapter for some resources while you're working out your plans in the first place.

Because scholarships and grants and the infinite rules surrounding financial aid change so often, I cannot include every possible source of funding for you and, therefore, won't even bother to try. What I *will* try to do is include major sources for conducting a search tailored to your needs.

You've already taken some of these steps by now since you've read previous chapters, but I will list some of the major sources for finding financial aid, scholarships, and grants that you can search through, figure out whether you qualify for, and apply to.

Start with financial aid. Head online to www.studentaid.gov to find up-to-date information relevant to your situation. You will also find links and instructions for applying for aid and loans here. You may ask for assistance from your new school or from a counselor at your high school.

In general (because every reader's case will vary), if you are offered some amount of grant money through financial aid but have to make up some amount in loans, you'll want to apply all over for scholarships to reduce that need. When you receive a scholarship, you must let your school know about it as soon as possible so they can reduce your loans. This also applies if you've received other aid, in which case the scholarship will probably reduce a federal grant if you have one. Scholarships and grants won in excess of the cost of attendance, and any loans or other monies you might have been granted from federal aid will become a refund from the school that you may need to pay taxes on. However, if you've been an incredibly diligent scholarship applicant and managed to do this, then congratulations to you!

Studentaid.gov provides some links to programs that will help you find and apply for suitable scholarships and grants. I want to point out the TRIO programs. You can find these either through the Studentaid.gov website or by conducting a simple online search for "student TRIO program." TRIO programs are designed for low-income students, students who are the first in their generation to go to college, and disabled students. There are a number of programs, and it's worth taking a few minutes to see whether you might fit into any of the categories they serve.

Another suggestion from Studentaid.gov is www.careeronestop.org, a government-sponsored program that assists in a number of life phases related to work, training, and education. Follow links on the main site for scholarships and financial aid for more information.

You may find specific grants that you could apply for from your state government. You should look into local businesses sponsoring scholarships. Sometimes, your local pizza shop might have a small scholarship for high school seniors to apply to, and companies you already work part-time for may also have scholarship/grant programs for employees. You should also check up on any scholarship or grant you may qualify for through any religious or community organization that you or your family belong to. If your family is (or was) in the military, you may find you qualify for certain financial programs.

Your new school will surely have some recommendations regarding scholarships and grants. You can also ask current students what they applied for. Your program may also have financial need, scholarship, or grant assistance available once you've been accepted.

Sites like Scholarships.com may be useful as well. Scholarships.com has been around for a long time and is free. Any scholarship search website should be free for you to search through. Please do thorough research on any scholarship site you may find, as the more popular sites will change over time—to the extent that not every listing here will remain accurate.

An excellent source for searching out scholarships and grants to apply for is your local or high school library. Librarians are the keepers of information and are always especially happy to help curious students who show up asking for guidance. You may even discover a section of pamphlets, brochures, advertisements, or other forms of information set up exclusively for financial assistance for higher education and training. Libraries might even be more likely to have useful information regarding training and certificate programs.

CHAPTER 11: WHAT'S NEXT: PREPARING FOR COLLEGE (BONUS CHAPTER)

Okay! Congratulations, you're on your way! What are you packing? What will your daily routine be like? What will your budget look like?

I'm sure by now you've already crafted some preliminary budgets in deciding what you can afford. However, now you have to make yourself a budget *for real* that you *stick to.* Which is hard. I know it's hard because I'm also living in this world of money. Sometimes, I just want the groceries to appear, the roof over my head to stay steady, and nothing to do with making that happen. That's a totally normal feeling, too. Of course, that's not particularly realistic for most people, and even if you're the wealthiest person on planet Earth, it's always possible to lose that status without a budget.

What goes into your budget?

Use software or make your own spreadsheet, making sure to consider these questions before you even begin to assign numbers to paper. Is it possible to have a car on campus, and if so, will you bring one? (And if you don't already own a vehicle, what will you spend to get one?) Can you live in a dorm, or will you need to lease or rent? (And which would be cheaper?) Will you be on a meal plan, and will it cover all or only some meals? Will you have access to a kitchen? Will you have a mini-fridge in your dorm room? (And will you own it or rent it?) Will you be headed somewhere with a completely different climate and need to add items to your wardrobe to avoid freezing or sweating to death? Will any extracurricular activities or sports teams require items you already own, or will you need to purchase them? (And will these things require maintenance?) Are there dues you might need to pay toward any clubs or memberships? (And will you set a spending limit for yourself on any clubs or memberships you might want to join?) Will you have space for any needed items for side gigs in whatever space you live in?

There are plenty more questions you should ask yourself that I might not even be able to think of for you, but that's a good start. I'm going to include a quick rundown of categories for your budget here, too. For any college-specific numbers in these categories, like the room and board expenses you will be charged if you live in a dorm, be sure to figure out the exact price for the year or semesters that you will be living on campus and the exact pricing for your specific room/living situation in whatever building you are assigned or able to pick out. Plenty of schools charge the same for a single-, double-, or triple-occupancy room across the whole campus, but some will also charge varying rates depending on which dormitory building you live in. Hopefully, those rates don't range too widely if you're struggling to craft a budget too far in advance, but it's still wise to have the precise costs ready whenever possible. Some of these may be one-time purchases required across your entire academic career (such as a computer or lifetime software licenses), whereas others will be more frequent:

* Rent/on-campus dorm expenses

* Utilities (if not included in dorm figures)

* Groceries (or meal plan or meal plan plus any groceries you'll have in your room)

* Health insurance (and any health-related items like vitamins, prescription costs, or medical devices)

* Dining out or ordering delivery (even the most avid home cook is going to order some greasy something at 2 a.m. when pulling an all-nighter, working, or partying at least once a semester)

* Textbooks/book rentals/supplies

* Lab fees

* Backpack/bag to carry whatever you need to class

* Personal care (serious question: Do you need to buy your own toilet paper?)

* Required technology (laptop or desktop computer, any software you might need that hopefully has an educational discount license, headphones, camera, microphone, accessories)

* Wardrobe (even the most shopping-averse people will sometimes discover they need new shoes, outerwear, underwear, or socks, so craft a small budget for that, even if it's just a once-a-year purchase)

* Transportation (car, car insurance, gasoline, maintenance on the car, emergency car breakdown fund, parking passes, local bus pass, and/or flight/train/bus home if you can't stay on campus over breaks)

* Emergency fund (for all the unexpected things that might pull at the money in your wallet or money that doesn't even exist in your wallet right now)

* Entertainment (set your budget for this as low as you can but stay realistic because I guarantee you'll want to go see a movie, pay for streaming video services, buy a book, head to a zoo, or whatever, and you really can't try to *never* do anything fun in college without fueling a meltdown)

* Savings (maybe this sounds silly now, but no matter how little you'll have left over in your budget, you should put it into a savings or investment account that will help it grow even a small amount)

Since your school will probably take payment for an entire semester out of your financial aid/loans if you get them, you can calculate what will be left over to live on. If you're able to afford the tuition and fees yourself or via your family, you'll have to figure out that number on your own. It's best to write down everything you can think of and give yourself a realistic and reasonable budget for costs that will vary, such as groceries, outings, and emergency costs. Don't pretend you'll only ever spend $10 beyond your meal plan if it doesn't cover every meal—and even if it does, you still might not be on campus to use it one day (and you still need to eat!).

My undergraduate (and graduate) days are pretty long ago now, but I think the following advice still applies: Try to have some amount of cash on you for purchases you may need to make. This is more an exercise in remembering that you're using real money and keeping the feeling of parting with it in your mind. If you have $100 in cash as a personal limit for the week, you'll really *feel* that spending and the loss of that $100 from your wallet versus the sliding, swiping, inserting, tapping, and waving games we do nowadays with cards. I used cards in my undergraduate years, too, of course, but the practice of keeping some amount of cash on me helped keep it "real."

I'm not a financial advisor or expert, but I would also recommend that you immediately begin finding ways to save and invest that fit your situation. Everyone —and I do mean everyone—should have some type of investment. Whether it makes more sense for you to have a simple savings account that accrues a very small percent of interest, buy some shorter-term bonds or CDs, or invest in stocks is up to you, but you should be doing something. The younger you start setting up your finances, the better. Find out now from your family whether there are any bonds or savings or trust funds that you will be due at any point in the future, assuming you don't already have access to these. I'm a couple of years away from 40, and I still have some bonds that my grandmother gifted me as a child that have not fully matured. These might be a great option if you're younger and can actually wait for them to mature. Either way, do your research and ask for help because interest rates on long-term bonds right now are not as good as they were thirty years ago, and you might find other investments that are more worthy of your money.

It might behoove you to find a free or low-cost stock investment app. I'm not affiliated with any of them, but I have used and continue to use several. Some will charge you a monthly fee to use their services. If you only have perhaps $100 a year to invest, you will likely lose money over time with any service that charges you even a dollar a month. However, there can also be benefits to the same services like free tiny portions of stock or random gifted stocks for referring a friend. You've got a lot on your plate as it is, so try to pick something that you won't need to think about too often while still giving you growth.

Even if you're studying business or finance and feel confident about investing, don't just "YOLO" your money into the latest popular scheme. Your risk tolerance is higher based on your age but not so high that you can afford to lose your loan money, grant money, scholarship money, or hard-earned paycheck and be stuck broke or in debt. If you feel comfortable investing in riskier stocks, cryptocurrencies, or other volatile investments, remember to be reasonable about what you're doing and keep a balanced portfolio of riskier choices and safer choices. You have plenty of time to create a strong portfolio for yourself or with financial advisors, so keep in mind that you're still at the novice level without a particularly high tolerance for risk, no matter how much money is currently sitting in your bank account.

Some other good general advice about managing your money is to utilize and build good credit without getting yourself in over your head. Having something like a PayPal Credit account with "promotions" that seem to constantly be active for no interest for a length of time (often six months) on purchases can also be useful as a backup for emergency and unforeseen costs. With any type of credit, do your research and be careful not to overspend. If you can't afford that expensive thing within a few months with or without interest, you can't afford it. However, if you have a need to take an emergency flight home, for example, finding ways to spread out pieces of that unexpected cost is a lot more approachable than simply going right into debt. There are legitimate ways out there to help build strong credit, including having a small credit card line that you use for basic costs and pay in full at the end of each month, that you should be utilizing to prepare for leasing an apartment, buying a house, leasing or buying a new or used car, etc. Credit can be really dangerous if you don't have a solid plan and know what you're doing, but it's also the key to unlocking many necessary things in the future, so take care to protect and manage it well, just as you would cash in your pocket.

One last thing to keep in mind about finances is to figure out whether you have time and energy for a part-time job, a side gig, or work-study. If you're already working at a franchised place or doing remote work online, you may have a part-time job that simply transfers along with you to your new location. If not, it may be worth searching for a flexible part-time job. If you can't find a flexible enough position or you're not comfortable committing too many work hours while starting your new education and daily routine, perhaps freelancing or side gigs are for you. Find reputable freelance sites or just put up some ads in your area for a dog walker and let clients call you about your availability. These are jobs that you can accept or decline at your discretion, and if you start to feel overwhelmed, you can easily discuss an end date for your gig with any clients. Work-study jobs may be a little more frustrating to land but should be very flexible about part-time hours. Work-study jobs are frequently simple tasks, but sometimes, especially once you've been on campus, getting to know your professors and becoming involved in your program, you may discover opportunities to be a teacher's assistant, conduct research in a science lab for a professor, or be a specialized technician of some sort. These will be nicer boosts to your resume than swiping ID cards at the dining hall and may even pay better, too, but all earnings can be helpful. Don't snub opportunities that you think you could actually do. You can always find better ones later, but with more work experience under your belt and more money in your wallet.

If you're preparing to live on campus, what will you be bringing with you? I don't want to evangelize being a minimalist, but from personal experience, the less you can bring with you, the better. When I went off to live in my single-room dorm for freshman year, my mother wanted me to bring what seemed like four thousand things. I had an iron and a small ironing board. Why? Because she thought I should be able to iron for any fancy occasion or interview or whatever I might have. Do you know how many times I used those things? Precisely zero. I didn't own clothes that required ironing, and I had very few occasions to wear anything fancy anyway. So, I've made you a list of categories of things you'll want to bring to help you when deciding how to fit your life necessities into whatever tiny space you'll be living in. For this list, I'm assuming you won't be moving into an unfurnished apartment. If that's the case for your first year, this list still is helpful, but you'll also want to add furniture and kitchen items:

* Weather-appropriate clothing and footwear and hangers

* Backpack or whatever bag you'll be using to carry books and/or tech

* Mini-fridge or mini-fridge/microwave combo. My parents gifted me with a combo rental in my freshman year that I cannot imagine having lived without. Having a setup for cold drinks, leftovers, groceries, and a means to pop popcorn, heat up canned soup, or reheat leftovers at any time of the day or night was a luxury that was worth every penny!

* Bedding (be sure to find out whether you need an extra-long twin set or some other special size of bedding for the dorm you'll be in)

* One or two extra blankets/throw blankets depending on how cold it is where you'll be

* Two or three oversized towels

* Robe

* Small shower basket to store and bring with you to the bathroom and showers if you share, or simply for easy storage if you have access to your own bathroom (in which case, you'll also want to have some bathroom cleaning supplies and your

own stock of hand soap and toilet paper)

* Computer and accessories and any other program-specific tech you may require. Ask yourself whether you'll need a printer depending on what your professors require. My concentration in undergrad was in screenwriting, and many projects required me to print out copies for my classmates of multiple pages, which I could do at the printing lab on campus, but it was a huge pain and took a lot of extra time, so it was something I avoided for smaller printing tasks by having a printer in my room.

* Personal tech or gear. I use my phone for pretty much everything now, but back in college, I brought my Discman (try not to judge me for being old!). This category should include anything you like to use that isn't specifically for school, like a television (perhaps a requirement for television and film majors), a tablet, a video game console (probably a requirement for game designers), headphones, musical instruments (digital or not—probably needed if you're a music major), and any sports equipment for a school team or simply because you love to play.

* A small assortment of dry groceries and/or storage for paper plates or one or two plates, bowls, cups, and utensils. Don't bring service for more than two people because the temptation to never wash a bunch of items will create significantly larger burdens than simply washing one or two

items soon after use.

* A few personal touches like photos, posters, or decorations. These are important to bring but can quickly contribute to clutter if you overdo it.

* An agenda planner that works for you. This could be a digital or physical planner. Either way, bring some means of keeping your schedule laid out while supporting good time management.

* An alarm clock—a *real* one. Hear me out, but waking up to the alarm on your phone is vastly different from waking up to an alarm clock on the other side of the room, especially when you're the only one remotely in charge of getting up on time. It's a better strategy to have a solid alarm clock with you than to rely on your phone.

This still adds up to quite a bit of stuff. A couple of extra tips: You may want shelf paper/liners to put into the drawers you get in your room or on the shelving provided. If your closet space is open-access with a hanging rod across it, you may consider setting up an adjustable spring rod and cheap shower curtain to create a cover for the closet (you can even change in there if you share a room with others and aren't claustrophobic). You might want a sturdy welcome mat to put your wet shoes on and perhaps even some small area rugs to keep your feet from getting cold. You'll also want a small vacuum and a smattering of cleaning supplies, even if you're only responsible for your room and no bathroom or kitchen. Disinfecting and wiping down any spills or messes on your desk is important, and trying to accomplish a cleaning task with some paper towels from the bathroom is never going to do as good a job or be as quick a task. If your school has a "Big Sib"-type program that pairs you with a current student, I encourage you to utilize this person's experience by asking whether they can come up with any good tips for dorm life, campus life, or any conveniences they would recommend. I believe my parents discovered the mini-fridge combo unit rental by asking questions at an Accepted Students Day presentation for parents. There are plenty of organic ways to get some information and personal experiences so that you can start out on a good, solid footing.

One final bit of advice on what to bring with you: Whatever you're doing, do it with integrity. I cannot emphasize enough how important integrity is in life. Life isn't fair, but you don't have to behave poorly as a result. You cannot control others, but you *can* control your own actions. You might not be able to control how you feel about things at first, but you *can* control what you choose to dwell on and how you respond to those feelings. People, especially in my age group and younger, have often grown up being told that hard work now means success later. That can be true, but it's not the best correlation. Plenty of successful people have not worked hard at all, and plenty of hard-working people have found little success in life. The feeling of sadness and disgust that this truth can create for me (and, surely, most people) can be mitigated somewhat by being assured of one's own integrity. If I've worked hard on something that didn't pan out to be as useful or great as I had hoped, I still feel some satisfaction that I didn't compromise my integrity in the process. People will notice when you behave with integrity, and it will help attract other people who behave with integrity into your life.

Remember to get good at time management (a skill everyone needs throughout their lives), take care of yourself mentally and physically, and be honest and respectful to others. If you want to be *really* prepared, you can also pick up a copy of my book *The Lazy Student's Guide to Writing Papers and Getting College Done Right: Work Smarter, Not Harder* in Kindle, physical, or audiobook format from Amazon.com.

Whatever you're off to do now, I believe in you. You can do this. If you liked this guide, be sure to give it a good review. If you have any questions or comments, you can contact me via my personal webstite at **www.juligriffo.com** or www.lastplutonian.com, the website for my company and publisher of this book. Thank you so much for reading my guidebook!

www.ingramcontent.com/pod-product-compliance
Lightning Source LLC
LaVergne TN
LVHW052258070426
835507LV00036B/3324